CATTLE KEEPING
Cow Calf Record Book

BUSINESS EMERGENCY CONTACTS

BUSINESS INFORMATION

BUSINESS NAME	
FACILITY NAME	
ADDRESS	
FACILITY PHONE 1	
FACILITY PHONE 2	

EMERGENCY NUMBERS

FIRE DEPT	
POLICE DEPT	
AMBULANCE SVC	
HOSPITAL	
POISON CONTROL	
ALARM COMPANY	

UTILITY COMPANIES

NATURAL GAS	
ELECTRICITY	
WATER SVC	

INSURANCE COMPANY

COMPANY NAME	
CLAIMS HOTLINE	
POLICY NUMBER	

UPDATE INFORMATION

UPDATED BY	
DATE OF UPDATE	

FACILITY MANAGERS

NAME	PRIMARY CONTACT	ALTERNATE

EMPLOYEES

NAME	PRIMARY CONTACT	ALTERNATE

Cow Production History

Cow ID:

Description (Breed/color):

Cow's Sire		Sire Breed	
Cow's Dam		Dam Breed	
Cow's Birth Date		Weaning Weight	
Purchase Date		Purchase Price	

Date of Sale or Removal	
Sale Weight	
Sale Price/lb	
Total Value	

Individual Cow Production Record

Calving

	Year	Bull ID & Breed	Cow Age	Calf ID	Calf Birth Date	Calf Sex	Birth Weight	Calving Ease	Calving Interval Days
1									
2									
3									
4									
5									
6									
7									
8									

Weaning

	Weaning Weight	205 Adj Wt.
1		
2		
3		
4		
5		
6		
7		
8		

Yearling

	Yearling Weight	365 Adj Wt.
1		
2		
3		
4		
5		
6		
7		
8		

Pregnant Test

	Pregnant (P) or (O) Open	BCS
1		
2		
3		
4		
5		
6		
7		
8		

Cow Production History

Cow ID	
Description (Breed/color)	

Cow's Sire		Sire Breed	
Cow's Dam		Dam Breed	
Cow's Birth Date		Weaning Weight	
Purchase Date		Purchase Price	

Date of Sale or Removal	
Sale Weight	
Sale Price/lb	
Total Value	

Individual Cow Production Record

Calving

	Year	Bull ID & Breed	Cow Age	Calf ID	Calf Birth Date	Calf Sex	Birth Weight	Calving Ease	Calving Interval Days
1									
2									
3									
4									
5									
6									
7									
8									

Weaning

	Weaning Weight	205 Adj Wt.
1		
2		
3		
4		
5		
6		
7		
8		

Yearling

	Yearling Weight	365 Adj Wt.
1		
2		
3		
4		
5		
6		
7		
8		

Pregnant Test

	Pregnant (P) or (O) Open	BCS
1		
2		
3		
4		
5		
6		
7		
8		

Cow Production History

Cow ID		Date of Sale or Removal	
Description (Breed/color)		Sale Weight	
Cow's Sire	Sire Breed	Sale Price/lb	
Cow's Dam	Dam Breed		
Cow's Birth Date	Weaning Weight	Total Value	
Purchase Date	Purchase Price		

Individual Cow Production Record

Calving

	Year	Bull ID & Breed	Cow Age	Calf ID	Calf Birth Date	Calf Sex	Birth Weight	Calving Ease	Calving Interval Days
1									
2									
3									
4									
5									
6									
7									
8									

Weaning

	Weaning Weight	205 Adj Wt.
1		
2		
3		
4		
5		
6		
7		
8		

Yearling

	Yearling Weight	365 Adj Wt.
1		
2		
3		
4		
5		
6		
7		
8		

Pregnant Test

	Pregnant (P) or (O) Open	BCS
1		
2		
3		
4		
5		
6		
7		
8		

Notes

Notes

Cow Production History

Cow ID [ ]

Description (Breed/color) [ ]

Cow's Sire [ ]	Sire Breed [ ]	Date of Sale or Removal	[ ]
Cow's Dam [ ]	Dam Breed [ ]	Sale Weight	[ ]
Cow's Birth Date [ ]	Weaning Weight [ ]	Sale Price/lb	[ ]
Purchase Date [ ]	Purchase Price [ ]	Total Value	[ ]

Individual Cow Production Record

Calving

	Year	Bull ID & Breed	Cow Age	Calf ID	Calf Birth Date	Calf Sex	Birth Weight	Calving Ease	Calving Interval Days
1									
2									
3									
4									
5									
6									
7									
8									

Weaning

	Weaning Weight	205 Adj Wt.
1		
2		
3		
4		
5		
6		
7		
8		

Yearling

	Yearling Weight	365 Adj Wt.
1		
2		
3		
4		
5		
6		
7		
8		

Pregnant Test

	Pregnant (P) or (O) Open	BCS
1		
2		
3		
4		
5		
6		
7		
8		

Cow Production History

Cow ID		Date of Sale or Removal	
Description (Breed/color)			

				Date of Sale or Removal	

Cow ID _____

Description (Breed/color) _____

Cow's Sire _____	Sire Breed _____		
Cow's Dam _____	Dam Breed _____		
Cow's Birth Date _____	Weaning Weight _____		
Purchase Date _____	Purchase Price _____		

Date of Sale or Removal	
Sale Weight	
Sale Price/lb	
Total Value	

Individual Cow Production Record

Calving									
Year	Bull ID & Breed	Cow Age	Calf ID	Calf Birth Date	Calf Sex	Birth Weight	Calving Ease	Calving Interval Days
1									
2									
3									
4									
5									
6									
7									
8									

Weaning	
Weaning Weight	205 Adj Wt.
1	
2	
3	
4	
5	
6	
7	
8	

Yearling	
Yearling Weight	365 Adj Wt.
1	
2	
3	
4	
5	
6	
7	
8	

Pregnant Test	
Pregnant (P) or (O) Open	BCS
1	
2	
3	
4	
5	
6	
7	
8	

Notes

Notes

Cow Production History

Cow ID		Date of Sale or Removal	

Description (Breed/color)

Cow's Sire		Sire Breed		Sale Weight	
Cow's Dam		Dam Breed		Sale Price/lb	
Cow's Birth Date		Weaning Weight		Total Value	
Purchase Date		Purchase Price			

Individual Cow Production Record

Calving

	Year	Bull ID & Breed	Cow Age	Calf ID	Calf Birth Date	Calf Sex	Birth Weight	Calving Ease	Calving Interval Days
1									
2									
3									
4									
5									
6									
7									
8									

Weaning

	Weaning Weight	205 Adj Wt.
1		
2		
3		
4		
5		
6		
7		
8		

Yearling

	Yearling Weight	365 Adj Wt.
1		
2		
3		
4		
5		
6		
7		
8		

Pregnant Test

	Pregnant (P) or (O) Open	BCS
1		
2		
3		
4		
5		
6		
7		
8		

Cow Production History

Cow ID		Date of Sale or Removal	
Description (Breed/color)		Sale Weight	
Cow's Sire	Sire Breed		
Cow's Dam	Dam Breed	Sale Price/lb	
Cow's Birth Date	Weaning Weight		
Purchase Date	Purchase Price	Total Value	

Individual Cow Production Record

Calving

	Year	Bull ID & Breed	Cow Age	Calf ID	Calf Birth Date	Calf Sex	Birth Weight	Calving Ease	Calving Interval Days
1									
2									
3									
4									
5									
6									
7									
8									

	Weaning		Yearling		Pregnant Test	
	Weaning Weight	205 Adj Wt.	Yearling Weight	365 Adj Wt.	Pregnant (P) or (O) Open	BCS
1						
2						
3						
4						
5						
6						
7						
8						

Notes

Notes

Cow Production History

Cow ID: _____

Description (Breed/color): _____

Cow's Sire	_____	Sire Breed	_____
Cow's Dam	_____	Dam Breed	_____
Cow's Birth Date	_____	Weaning Weight	_____
Purchase Date	_____	Purchase Price	_____

Date of Sale or Removal	
Sale Weight	
Sale Price/lb	
Total Value	

Individual Cow Production Record

Calving

	Year	Bull ID & Breed	Cow Age	Calf ID	Calf Birth Date	Calf Sex	Birth Weight	Calving Ease	Calving Interval Days
1									
2									
3									
4									
5									
6									
7									
8									

Weaning

	Weaning Weight	205 Adj Wt.
1		
2		
3		
4		
5		
6		
7		
8		

Yearling

	Yearling Weight	365 Adj Wt.
1		
2		
3		
4		
5		
6		
7		
8		

Pregnant Test

	Pregnant (P) or (O) Open	BCS
1		
2		
3		
4		
5		
6		
7		
8		

Cow Production History

Cow ID	
Description (Breed/color)	

Cow's Sire		Sire Breed	
Cow's Dam		Dam Breed	
Cow's Birth Date		Weaning Weight	
Purchase Date		Purchase Price	

Date of Sale or Removal	
Sale Weight	
Sale Price/lb	
Total Value	

Individual Cow Production Record

Calving

	Year	Bull ID & Breed	Cow Age	Calf ID	Calf Birth Date	Calf Sex	Birth Weight	Calving Ease	Calving Interval Days
1									
2									
3									
4									
5									
6									
7									
8									

Weaning

	Weaning Weight	205 Adj Wt.
1		
2		
3		
4		
5		
6		
7		
8		

Yearling

	Yearling Weight	365 Adj Wt.
1		
2		
3		
4		
5		
6		
7		
8		

Pregnant Test

	Pregnant (P) or (O) Open	BCS
1		
2		
3		
4		
5		
6		
7		
8		

Notes

Notes

Cow Production History

Cow ID		Date of Sale or Removal	
Description (Breed/color)		Sale Weight	
Cow's Sire	Sire Breed	Sale Price/lb	
Cow's Dam	Dam Breed		
Cow's Birth Date	Weaning Weight	Total Value	
Purchase Date	Purchase Price		

Individual Cow Production Record

Calving

	Year	Bull ID & Breed	Cow Age	Calf ID	Calf Birth Date	Calf Sex	Birth Weight	Calving Ease	Calving Interval Days
1									
2									
3									
4									
5									
6									
7									
8									

Weaning

	Weaning Weight	205 Adj Wt.
1		
2		
3		
4		
5		
6		
7		
8		

Yearling

	Yearling Weight	365 Adj Wt.
1		
2		
3		
4		
5		
6		
7		
8		

Pregnant Test

	Pregnant (P) or (O) Open	BCS
1		
2		
3		
4		
5		
6		
7		
8		

Cow Production History

Cow ID [   ]

Description (Breed/color) [   ]

Cow's Sire [ ]	Sire Breed [ ]		Date of Sale or Removal	
Cow's Dam [ ]	Dam Breed [ ]		Sale Weight	
Cow's Birth Date [ ]	Weaning Weight [ ]		Sale Price/lb	
Purchase Date [ ]	Purchase Price [ ]		Total Value	

Individual Cow Production Record

Calving

	Year	Bull ID & Breed	Cow Age	Calf ID	Calf Birth Date	Calf Sex	Birth Weight	Calving Ease	Calving Interval Days
1									
2									
3									
4									
5									
6									
7									
8									

Weaning

	Weaning Weight	205 Adj Wt.
1		
2		
3		
4		
5		
6		
7		
8		

Yearling

	Yearling Weight	365 Adj Wt.
1		
2		
3		
4		
5		
6		
7		
8		

Pregnant Test

	Pregnant (P) or (O) Open	BCS
1		
2		
3		
4		
5		
6		
7		
8		

Notes

Notes

Cow Production History

Cow ID [   ]

Description (Breed/color) [   ]

Cow's Sire [   ]   Sire Breed [   ]

Cow's Dam [   ]   Dam Breed [   ]

Cow's Birth Date [   ]   Weaning Weight [   ]

Purchase Date [   ]   Purchase Price [   ]

Date of Sale or Removal	
Sale Weight	
Sale Price/lb	
Total Value	

Individual Cow Production Record

Calving

	Year	Bull ID & Breed	Cow Age	Calf ID	Calf Birth Date	Calf Sex	Birth Weight	Calving Ease	Calving Interval Days
1									
2									
3									
4									
5									
6									
7									
8									

Weaning		Yearling		Pregnant Test	
Weaning Weight	205 Adj Wt.	Yearling Weight	365 Adj Wt.	Pregnant (P) or (O) Open	BCS

Cow Production History

Cow ID [_____]

Description (Breed/color) [_____]

Cow's Sire [_____]	Sire Breed [_____]	
Cow's Dam [_____]	Dam Breed [_____]	
Cow's Birth Date [_____]	Weaning Weight [_____]	
Purchase Date [_____]	Purchase Price [_____]	

Date of Sale or Removal	
Sale Weight	
Sale Price/lb	
Total Value	

Individual Cow Production Record

Calving

	Year	Bull ID & Breed	Cow Age	Calf ID	Calf Birth Date	Calf Sex	Birth Weight	Calving Ease	Calving Interval Days
1									
2									
3									
4									
5									
6									
7									
8									

Weaning

	Weaning Weight	205 Adj Wt.
1		
2		
3		
4		
5		
6		
7		
8		

Yearling

	Yearling Weight	365 Adj Wt.
1		
2		
3		
4		
5		
6		
7		
8		

Pregnant Test

	Pregnant (P) or (O) Open	BCS
1		
2		
3		
4		
5		
6		
7		
8		

Notes

Notes

Cow Production History

Cow ID _____

Description (Breed/color) _____

Cow's Sire _____ Sire Breed _____

Cow's Dam _____ Dam Breed _____

Cow's Birth Date _____ Weaning Weight _____

Purchase Date _____ Purchase Price _____

Date of Sale or Removal	
Sale Weight	
Sale Price/lb	
Total Value	

Individual Cow Production Record

Calving									
Year	Bull ID & Breed	Cow Age	Calf ID	Calf Birth Date	Calf Sex	Birth Weight	Calving Ease	Calving Interval Days
1									
2									
3									
4									
5									
6									
7									
8									

Weaning		Yearling		Pregnant Test	
Weaning Weight	205 Adj Wt.	Yearling Weight	365 Adj Wt.	Pregnant (P) or (O) Open	BCS
1					
2					
3					
4					
5					
6					
7					
8					

Cow Production History

Cow ID		Date of Sale or Removal	
Description (Breed/color)			
Cow's Sire	Sire Breed	Sale Weight	
Cow's Dam	Dam Breed	Sale Price/lb	
Cow's Birth Date	Weaning Weight		
Purchase Date	Purchase Price	Total Value	

Individual Cow Production Record

Calving

	Year	Bull ID & Breed	Cow Age	Calf ID	Calf Birth Date	Calf Sex	Birth Weight	Calving Ease	Calving Interval Days
1									
2									
3									
4									
5									
6									
7									
8									

	Weaning		Yearling		Pregnant Test	
	Weaning Weight	205 Adj Wt.	Yearling Weight	365 Adj Wt.	Pregnant (P) or (O) Open	BCS
1						
2						
3						
4						
5						
6						
7						
8						

Notes

Notes

Cow Production History

Cow ID _____

Description (Breed/color) _____

Cow's Sire _____ Sire Breed _____

Cow's Dam _____ Dam Breed _____

Cow's Birth Date _____ Weaning Weight _____

Purchase Date _____ Purchase Price _____

Date of Sale or Removal	
Sale Weight	
Sale Price/lb	
Total Value	

Individual Cow Production Record

Calving

	Year	Bull ID & Breed	Cow Age	Calf ID	Calf Birth Date	Calf Sex	Birth Weight	Calving Ease	Calving Interval Days
1									
2									
3									
4									
5									
6									
7									
8									

Weaning

	Weaning Weight	205 Adj Wt.
1		
2		
3		
4		
5		
6		
7		
8		

Yearling

	Yearling Weight	365 Adj Wt.
1		
2		
3		
4		
5		
6		
7		
8		

Pregnant Test

	Pregnant (P) or (O) Open	BCS
1		
2		
3		
4		
5		
6		
7		
8		

Cow Production History

Cow ID	
Description (Breed/color)	

Cow's Sire		Sire Breed	
Cow's Dam		Dam Breed	
Cow's Birth Date		Weaning Weight	
Purchase Date		Purchase Price	

Date of Sale or Removal	
Sale Weight	
Sale Price/lb	
Total Value	

Individual Cow Production Record

Calving

	Year	Bull ID & Breed	Cow Age	Calf ID	Calf Birth Date	Calf Sex	Birth Weight	Calving Ease	Calving Interval Days
1									
2									
3									
4									
5									
6									
7									
8									

Weaning

	Weaning Weight	205 Adj Wt.
1		
2		
3		
4		
5		
6		
7		
8		

Yearling

	Yearling Weight	365 Adj Wt.
1		
2		
3		
4		
5		
6		
7		
8		

Pregnant Test

	Pregnant (P) or (O) Open	BCS
1		
2		
3		
4		
5		
6		
7		
8		

Notes

Notes

Cow Production History

Cow ID	
Description (Breed/color)	

Cow's Sire		Sire Breed	
Cow's Dam		Dam Breed	
Cow's Birth Date		Weaning Weight	
Purchase Date		Purchase Price	

Date of Sale or Removal	
Sale Weight	
Sale Price/lb	
Total Value	

Individual Cow Production Record

Calving

	Year	Bull ID & Breed	Cow Age	Calf ID	Calf Birth Date	Calf Sex	Birth Weight	Calving Ease	Calving Interval Days
1									
2									
3									
4									
5									
6									
7									
8									

Weaning

	Weaning Weight	205 Adj Wt.
1		
2		
3		
4		
5		
6		
7		
8		

Yearling

	Yearling Weight	365 Adj Wt.
1		
2		
3		
4		
5		
6		
7		
8		

Pregnant Test

	Pregnant (P) or (O) Open	BCS
1		
2		
3		
4		
5		
6		
7		
8		

Cow Production History

Cow ID		Date of Sale or Removal	
Description (Breed/color)		Sale Weight	
Cow's Sire	Sire Breed	Sale Price/lb	
Cow's Dam	Dam Breed		
Cow's Birth Date	Weaning Weight	Total Value	
Purchase Date	Purchase Price		

Individual Cow Production Record

Calving

	Year	Bull ID & Breed	Cow Age	Calf ID	Calf Birth Date	Calf Sex	Birth Weight	Calving Ease	Calving Interval Days
1									
2									
3									
4									
5									
6									
7									
8									

Weaning

	Weaning Weight	205 Adj Wt.
1		
2		
3		
4		
5		
6		
7		
8		

Yearling

	Yearling Weight	365 Adj Wt.
1		
2		
3		
4		
5		
6		
7		
8		

Pregnant Test

	Pregnant (P) or (O) Open	BCS
1		
2		
3		
4		
5		
6		
7		
8		

Notes

Notes

Cow Production History

Cow ID [   ]

Description (Breed/color) [   ]

Cow's Sire [   ]   Sire Breed [   ]

Cow's Dam [   ]   Dam Breed [   ]

Cow's Birth Date [   ]   Weaning Weight [   ]

Purchase Date [   ]   Purchase Price [   ]

Date of Sale or Removal	
Sale Weight	
Sale Price/lb	
Total Value	

Individual Cow Production Record

Calving

	Year	Bull ID & Breed	Cow Age	Calf ID	Calf Birth Date	Calf Sex	Birth Weight	Calving Ease	Calving Interval Days
1									
2									
3									
4									
5									
6									
7									
8									

Weaning

	Weaning Weight	205 Adj Wt.
1		
2		
3		
4		
5		
6		
7		
8		

Yearling

	Yearling Weight	365 Adj Wt.
1		
2		
3		
4		
5		
6		
7		
8		

Pregnant Test

	Pregnant (P) or (O) Open	BCS
1		
2		
3		
4		
5		
6		
7		
8		

Cow Production History

Cow ID	
Description (Breed/color)	
Cow's Sire	Sire Breed
Cow's Dam	Dam Breed
Cow's Birth Date	Weaning Weight
Purchase Date	Purchase Price

Date of Sale or Removal	
Sale Weight	
Sale Price/lb	
Total Value	

Individual Cow Production Record

Calving

	Year	Bull ID & Breed	Cow Age	Calf ID	Calf Birth Date	Calf Sex	Birth Weight	Calving Ease	Calving Interval Days
1									
2									
3									
4									
5									
6									
7									
8									

Weaning

	Weaning Weight	205 Adj Wt.
1		
2		
3		
4		
5		
6		
7		
8		

Yearling

	Yearling Weight	365 Adj Wt.
1		
2		
3		
4		
5		
6		
7		
8		

Pregnant Test

	Pregnant (P) or (O) Open	BCS
1		
2		
3		
4		
5		
6		
7		
8		

Notes

Notes

Cow Production History

Cow ID [   ]

Description (Breed/color) [   ]

			Date of Sale or Removal	
Cow's Sire [ ]	Sire Breed [ ]		Sale Weight	
Cow's Dam [ ]	Dam Breed [ ]		Sale Price/lb	
Cow's Birth Date [ ]	Weaning Weight [ ]		Total Value	
Purchase Date [ ]	Purchase Price [ ]			

Individual Cow Production Record

Calving

	Year	Bull ID & Breed	Cow Age	Calf ID	Calf Birth Date	Calf Sex	Birth Weight	Calving Ease	Calving Interval Days
1									
2									
3									
4									
5									
6									
7									
8									

Weaning

	Weaning Weight	205 Adj Wt.
1		
2		
3		
4		
5		
6		
7		
8		

Yearling

	Yearling Weight	365 Adj Wt.
1		
2		
3		
4		
5		
6		
7		
8		

Pregnant Test

	Pregnant (P) or (O) Open	BCS
1		
2		
3		
4		
5		
6		
7		
8		

Cow Production History

Cow ID		Date of Sale or Removal	
Description (Breed/color)		Sale Weight	
Cow's Sire	Sire Breed	Sale Price/lb	
Cow's Dam	Dam Breed		
Cow's Birth Date	Weaning Weight	Total Value	
Purchase Date	Purchase Price		

Individual Cow Production Record

Calving

	Year	Bull ID & Breed	Cow Age	Calf ID	Calf Birth Date	Calf Sex	Birth Weight	Calving Ease	Calving Interval Days
1									
2									
3									
4									
5									
6									
7									
8									

Weaning

	Weaning Weight	205 Adj Wt.
1		
2		
3		
4		
5		
6		
7		
8		

Yearling

	Yearling Weight	365 Adj Wt.
1		
2		
3		
4		
5		
6		
7		
8		

Pregnant Test

	Pregnant (P) or (O) Open	BCS
1		
2		
3		
4		
5		
6		
7		
8		

Notes

Notes

Cow Production History

Cow ID	
Description (Breed/color)	

Cow's Sire		Sire Breed	
Cow's Dam		Dam Breed	
Cow's Birth Date		Weaning Weight	
Purchase Date		Purchase Price	

Date of Sale or Removal	
Sale Weight	
Sale Price/lb	
Total Value	

Individual Cow Production Record

Calving

	Year	Bull ID & Breed	Cow Age	Calf ID	Calf Birth Date	Calf Sex	Birth Weight	Calving Ease	Calving Interval Days
1									
2									
3									
4									
5									
6									
7									
8									

Weaning

	Weaning Weight	205 Adj Wt.
1		
2		
3		
4		
5		
6		
7		
8		

Yearling

	Yearling Weight	365 Adj Wt.
1		
2		
3		
4		
5		
6		
7		
8		

Pregnant Test

	Pregnant (P) or (O) Open	BCS
1		
2		
3		
4		
5		
6		
7		
8		

Cow Production History

Cow ID	
Description (Breed/color)	
Cow's Sire	Sire Breed
Cow's Dam	Dam Breed
Cow's Birth Date	Weaning Weight
Purchase Date	Purchase Price

Date of Sale or Removal	
Sale Weight	
Sale Price/lb	
Total Value	

Individual Cow Production Record

Calving

	Year	Bull ID & Breed	Cow Age	Calf ID	Calf Birth Date	Calf Sex	Birth Weight	Calving Ease	Calving Interval Days
1									
2									
3									
4									
5									
6									
7									
8									

Weaning

	Weaning Weight	205 Adj Wt.
1		
2		
3		
4		
5		
6		
7		
8		

Yearling

	Yearling Weight	365 Adj Wt.
1		
2		
3		
4		
5		
6		
7		
8		

Pregnant Test

	Pregnant (P) or (O) Open	BCS
1		
2		
3		
4		
5		
6		
7		
8		

Notes

Notes

Cow Production History

Cow ID		Date of Sale or Removal	
Description (Breed/color)		Sale Weight	
Cow's Sire	Sire Breed	Sale Price/lb	
Cow's Dam	Dam Breed	Total Value	
Cow's Birth Date	Weaning Weight		
Purchase Date	Purchase Price		

Individual Cow Production Record

Calving

	Year	Bull ID & Breed	Cow Age	Calf ID	Calf Birth Date	Calf Sex	Birth Weight	Calving Ease	Calving Interval Days
1									
2									
3									
4									
5									
6									
7									
8									

Weaning

	Weaning Weight	205 Adj Wt.
1		
2		
3		
4		
5		
6		
7		
8		

Yearling

	Yearling Weight	365 Adj Wt.
1		
2		
3		
4		
5		
6		
7		
8		

Pregnant Test

	Pregnant (P) or (O) Open	BCS
1		
2		
3		
4		
5		
6		
7		
8		

Cow Production History

Cow ID _____

Description (Breed/color) _____

Cow's Sire _____	Sire Breed _____	
Cow's Dam _____	Dam Breed _____	
Cow's Birth Date _____	Weaning Weight _____	
Purchase Date _____	Purchase Price _____	

Date of Sale or Removal	
Sale Weight	
Sale Price/lb	
Total Value	

Individual Cow Production Record

Calving

	Year	Bull ID & Breed	Cow Age	Calf ID	Calf Birth Date	Calf Sex	Birth Weight	Calving Ease	Calving Interval Days
1									
2									
3									
4									
5									
6									
7									
8									

Weaning

	Weaning Weight	205 Adj Wt.
1		
2		
3		
4		
5		
6		
7		
8		

Yearling

	Yearling Weight	365 Adj Wt.
1		
2		
3		
4		
5		
6		
7		
8		

Pregnant Test

	Pregnant (P) or (O) Open	BCS
1		
2		
3		
4		
5		
6		
7		
8		

Notes

Notes

Cow Production History

Cow ID [   ]

Description (Breed/color) [   ]

Cow's Sire	[ ]	Sire Breed	[ ]	
Cow's Dam	[ ]	Dam Breed	[ ]	
Cow's Birth Date	[ ]	Weaning Weight	[ ]	
Purchase Date	[ ]	Purchase Price	[ ]	

Date of Sale or Removal	
Sale Weight	
Sale Price/lb	
Total Value	

Individual Cow Production Record

Calving

	Year	Bull ID & Breed	Cow Age	Calf ID	Calf Birth Date	Calf Sex	Birth Weight	Calving Ease	Calving Interval Days
1									
2									
3									
4									
5									
6									
7									
8									

Weaning

	Weaning Weight	205 Adj Wt.
1		
2		
3		
4		
5		
6		
7		
8		

Yearling

	Yearling Weight	365 Adj Wt.
1		
2		
3		
4		
5		
6		
7		
8		

Pregnant Test

	Pregnant (P) or (O) Open	BCS
1		
2		
3		
4		
5		
6		
7		
8		

Cow Production History

Cow ID	
Description (Breed/color)	

Cow's Sire		Sire Breed	
Cow's Dam		Dam Breed	
Cow's Birth Date		Weaning Weight	
Purchase Date		Purchase Price	

Date of Sale or Removal	
Sale Weight	
Sale Price/lb	
Total Value	

Individual Cow Production Record

Calving

	Year	Bull ID & Breed	Cow Age	Calf ID	Calf Birth Date	Calf Sex	Birth Weight	Calving Ease	Calving Interval Days
1									
2									
3									
4									
5									
6									
7									
8									

Weaning

	Weaning Weight	205 Adj Wt.
1		
2		
3		
4		
5		
6		
7		
8		

Yearling

	Yearling Weight	365 Adj Wt.
1		
2		
3		
4		
5		
6		
7		
8		

Pregnant Test

	Pregnant (P) or (O) Open	BCS
1		
2		
3		
4		
5		
6		
7		
8		

Notes

Notes

Cow Production History

Cow ID

Description (Breed/color)

Cow's Sire _____   Sire Breed _____

Cow's Dam _____   Dam Breed _____

Cow's Birth Date _____   Weaning Weight _____

Purchase Date _____   Purchase Price _____

Date of Sale or Removal	
Sale Weight	
Sale Price/lb	
Total Value	

Individual Cow Production Record

Calving

	Year	Bull ID & Breed	Cow Age	Calf ID	Calf Birth Date	Calf Sex	Birth Weight	Calving Ease	Calving Interval Days
1									
2									
3									
4									
5									
6									
7									
8									

Weaning

	Weaning Weight	205 Adj Wt.
1		
2		
3		
4		
5		
6		
7		
8		

Yearling

	Yearling Weight	365 Adj Wt.
1		
2		
3		
4		
5		
6		
7		
8		

Pregnant Test

	Pregnant (P) or (O) Open	BCS
1		
2		
3		
4		
5		
6		
7		
8		

Cow Production History

Cow ID	
Description (Breed/color)	

Cow's Sire		Sire Breed	
Cow's Dam		Dam Breed	
Cow's Birth Date		Weaning Weight	
Purchase Date		Purchase Price	

Date of Sale or Removal	
Sale Weight	
Sale Price/lb	
Total Value	

Individual Cow Production Record

Calving

	Year	Bull ID & Breed	Cow Age	Calf ID	Calf Birth Date	Calf Sex	Birth Weight	Calving Ease	Calving Interval Days
1									
2									
3									
4									
5									
6									
7									
8									

Weaning

	Weaning Weight	205 Adj Wt.
1		
2		
3		
4		
5		
6		
7		
8		

Yearling

	Yearling Weight	365 Adj Wt.
1		
2		
3		
4		
5		
6		
7		
8		

Pregnant Test

	Pregnant (P) or (O) Open	BCS
1		
2		
3		
4		
5		
6		
7		
8		

Notes

Notes

Cow Production History

Cow ID	
Description (Breed/color)	
Cow's Sire	Sire Breed
Cow's Dam	Dam Breed
Cow's Birth Date	Weaning Weight
Purchase Date	Purchase Price

Date of Sale or Removal	
Sale Weight	
Sale Price/lb	
Total Value	

Individual Cow Production Record

Calving

	Year	Bull ID & Breed	Cow Age	Calf ID	Calf Birth Date	Calf Sex	Birth Weight	Calving Ease	Calving Interval Days
1									
2									
3									
4									
5									
6									
7									
8									

Weaning

	Weaning Weight	205 Adj Wt.
1		
2		
3		
4		
5		
6		
7		
8		

Yearling

	Yearling Weight	365 Adj Wt.
1		
2		
3		
4		
5		
6		
7		
8		

Pregnant Test

	Pregnant (P) or (O) Open	BCS
1		
2		
3		
4		
5		
6		
7		
8		

Cow Production History

Cow ID		Date of Sale or Removal	
Description (Breed/color)		Sale Weight	
Cow's Sire	Sire Breed	Sale Price/lb	
Cow's Dam	Dam Breed		
Cow's Birth Date	Weaning Weight	Total Value	
Purchase Date	Purchase Price		

Individual Cow Production Record

Calving

	Year	Bull ID & Breed	Cow Age	Calf ID	Calf Birth Date	Calf Sex	Birth Weight	Calving Ease	Calving Interval Days
1									
2									
3									
4									
5									
6									
7									
8									

Weaning

	Weaning Weight	205 Adj Wt.
1		
2		
3		
4		
5		
6		
7		
8		

Yearling

	Yearling Weight	365 Adj Wt.
1		
2		
3		
4		
5		
6		
7		
8		

Pregnant Test

	Pregnant (P) or (O) Open	BCS
1		
2		
3		
4		
5		
6		
7		
8		

Notes

Notes

Cow Production History

Cow ID		Date of Sale or Removal	
Description (Breed/color)		Sale Weight	
Cow's Sire	Sire Breed		
Cow's Dam	Dam Breed	Sale Price/lb	
Cow's Birth Date	Weaning Weight		
Purchase Date	Purchase Price	Total Value	

Individual Cow Production Record

Calving

	Year	Bull ID & Breed	Cow Age	Calf ID	Calf Birth Date	Calf Sex	Birth Weight	Calving Ease	Calving Interval Days
1									
2									
3									
4									
5									
6									
7									
8									

Weaning

	Weaning Weight	205 Adj Wt.
1		
2		
3		
4		
5		
6		
7		
8		

Yearling

	Yearling Weight	365 Adj Wt.
1		
2		
3		
4		
5		
6		
7		
8		

Pregnant Test

	Pregnant (P) or (O) Open	BCS
1		
2		
3		
4		
5		
6		
7		
8		

Cow Production History

Cow ID	
Description (Breed/color)	

Cow's Sire		Sire Breed	
Cow's Dam		Dam Breed	
Cow's Birth Date		Weaning Weight	
Purchase Date		Purchase Price	

Date of Sale or Removal	
Sale Weight	
Sale Price/lb	
Total Value	

Individual Cow Production Record

Calving

	Year	Bull ID & Breed	Cow Age	Calf ID	Calf Birth Date	Calf Sex	Birth Weight	Calving Ease	Calving Interval Days
1									
2									
3									
4									
5									
6									
7									
8									

Weaning

	Weaning Weight	205 Adj Wt.
1		
2		
3		
4		
5		
6		
7		
8		

Yearling

	Yearling Weight	365 Adj Wt.
1		
2		
3		
4		
5		
6		
7		
8		

Pregnant Test

	Pregnant (P) or (O) Open	BCS
1		
2		
3		
4		
5		
6		
7		
8		

Notes

Notes

Cow Production History

Cow ID _____

Description (Breed/color) _____

Cow's Sire _____	Sire Breed _____		
Cow's Dam _____	Dam Breed _____		
Cow's Birth Date _____	Weaning Weight _____		
Purchase Date _____	Purchase Price _____		

Date of Sale or Removal	
Sale Weight	
Sale Price/lb	
Total Value	

Individual Cow Production Record

Calving

	Year	Bull ID & Breed	Cow Age	Calf ID	Calf Birth Date	Calf Sex	Birth Weight	Calving Ease	Calving Interval Days
1									
2									
3									
4									
5									
6									
7									
8									

Weaning

	Weaning Weight	205 Adj Wt.
1		
2		
3		
4		
5		
6		
7		
8		

Yearling

	Yearling Weight	365 Adj Wt.
1		
2		
3		
4		
5		
6		
7		
8		

Pregnant Test

	Pregnant (P) or (O) Open	BCS
1		
2		
3		
4		
5		
6		
7		
8		

Cow Production History

Cow ID	
Description (Breed/color)	
Cow's Sire	Sire Breed
Cow's Dam	Dam Breed
Cow's Birth Date	Weaning Weight
Purchase Date	Purchase Price

Date of Sale or Removal	
Sale Weight	
Sale Price/lb	
Total Value	

Individual Cow Production Record

Calving

	Year	Bull ID & Breed	Cow Age	Calf ID	Calf Birth Date	Calf Sex	Birth Weight	Calving Ease	Calving Interval Days
1									
2									
3									
4									
5									
6									
7									
8									

Weaning

	Weaning Weight	205 Adj Wt.
1		
2		
3		
4		
5		
6		
7		
8		

Yearling

	Yearling Weight	365 Adj Wt.
1		
2		
3		
4		
5		
6		
7		
8		

Pregnant Test

	Pregnant (P) or (O) Open	BCS
1		
2		
3		
4		
5		
6		
7		
8		

Notes

Notes

Cow Production History

Cow ID	
Description (Breed/color)	
Cow's Sire	Sire Breed
Cow's Dam	Dam Breed
Cow's Birth Date	Weaning Weight
Purchase Date	Purchase Price

Date of Sale or Removal	
Sale Weight	
Sale Price/lb	
Total Value	

Individual Cow Production Record

Calving

	Year	Bull ID & Breed	Cow Age	Calf ID	Calf Birth Date	Calf Sex	Birth Weight	Calving Ease	Calving Interval Days
1									
2									
3									
4									
5									
6									
7									
8									

Weaning

	Weaning Weight	205 Adj Wt.
1		
2		
3		
4		
5		
6		
7		
8		

Yearling

	Yearling Weight	365 Adj Wt.
1		
2		
3		
4		
5		
6		
7		
8		

Pregnant Test

	Pregnant (P) or (O) Open	BCS
1		
2		
3		
4		
5		
6		
7		
8		

Cow Production History

Cow ID _____

Description (Breed/color) _____

Cow's Sire _____ Sire Breed _____

Cow's Dam _____ Dam Breed _____

Cow's Birth Date _____ Weaning Weight _____

Purchase Date _____ Purchase Price _____

Date of Sale or Removal	
Sale Weight	
Sale Price/lb	
Total Value	

Individual Cow Production Record

Calving

	Year	Bull ID & Breed	Cow Age	Calf ID	Calf Birth Date	Calf Sex	Birth Weight	Calving Ease	Calving Interval Days
1									
2									
3									
4									
5									
6									
7									
8									

Weaning

	Weaning Weight	205 Adj Wt.
1		
2		
3		
4		
5		
6		
7		
8		

Yearling

	Yearling Weight	365 Adj Wt.
1		
2		
3		
4		
5		
6		
7		
8		

Pregnant Test

	Pregnant (P) or (O) Open	BCS
1		
2		
3		
4		
5		
6		
7		
8		

Notes

Notes

Cow Production History

Cow ID	
Description (Breed/color)	

Cow's Sire		Sire Breed	
Cow's Dam		Dam Breed	
Cow's Birth Date		Weaning Weight	
Purchase Date		Purchase Price	

Date of Sale or Removal	
Sale Weight	
Sale Price/lb	
Total Value	

Individual Cow Production Record

Calving

	Year	Bull ID & Breed	Cow Age	Calf ID	Calf Birth Date	Calf Sex	Birth Weight	Calving Ease	Calving Interval Days
1									
2									
3									
4									
5									
6									
7									
8									

Weaning

	Weaning Weight	205 Adj Wt.
1		
2		
3		
4		
5		
6		
7		
8		

Yearling

	Yearling Weight	365 Adj Wt.
1		
2		
3		
4		
5		
6		
7		
8		

Pregnant Test

	Pregnant (P) or (O) Open	BCS
1		
2		
3		
4		
5		
6		
7		
8		

Cow Production History

Cow ID		Date of Sale or Removal	
Description (Breed/color)		Sale Weight	

Cow's Sire		Sire Breed		Sale Weight	
Cow's Dam		Dam Breed		Sale Price/lb	
Cow's Birth Date		Weaning Weight		Total Value	
Purchase Date		Purchase Price			

Individual Cow Production Record

Calving

	Year	Bull ID & Breed	Cow Age	Calf ID	Calf Birth Date	Calf Sex	Birth Weight	Calving Ease	Calving Interval Days
1									
2									
3									
4									
5									
6									
7									
8									

Weaning

	Weaning Weight	205 Adj Wt.
1		
2		
3		
4		
5		
6		
7		
8		

Yearling

	Yearling Weight	365 Adj Wt.
1		
2		
3		
4		
5		
6		
7		
8		

Pregnant Test

	Pregnant (P) or (O) Open	BCS
1		
2		
3		
4		
5		
6		
7		
8		

Notes

Notes

Cow Production History

Cow ID		Date of Sale or Removal	
Description (Breed/color)		Sale Weight	
Cow's Sire	Sire Breed	Sale Price/lb	
Cow's Dam	Dam Breed		
Cow's Birth Date	Weaning Weight	Total Value	
Purchase Date	Purchase Price		

Individual Cow Production Record

Calving									
Year	Bull ID & Breed	Cow Age	Calf ID	Calf Birth Date	Calf Sex	Birth Weight	Calving Ease	Calving Interval Days
1									
2									
3									
4									
5									
6									
7									
8									

Weaning	
Weaning Weight	205 Adj Wt.
1	
2	
3	
4	
5	
6	
7	
8	

Yearling	
Yearling Weight	365 Adj Wt.
1	
2	
3	
4	
5	
6	
7	
8	

Pregnant Test	
Pregnant (P) or (O) Open	BCS
1	
2	
3	
4	
5	
6	
7	
8	

Cow Production History

Cow ID	
Description (Breed/color)	

Cow's Sire		Sire Breed	
Cow's Dam		Dam Breed	
Cow's Birth Date		Weaning Weight	
Purchase Date		Purchase Price	

Date of Sale or Removal	
Sale Weight	
Sale Price/lb	
Total Value	

Individual Cow Production Record

Calving

	Year	Bull ID & Breed	Cow Age	Calf ID	Calf Birth Date	Calf Sex	Birth Weight	Calving Ease	Calving Interval Days
1									
2									
3									
4									
5									
6									
7									
8									

Weaning

	Weaning Weight	205 Adj Wt.
1		
2		
3		
4		
5		
6		
7		
8		

Yearling

	Yearling Weight	365 Adj Wt.
1		
2		
3		
4		
5		
6		
7		
8		

Pregnant Test

	Pregnant (P) or (O) Open	BCS
1		
2		
3		
4		
5		
6		
7		
8		

Notes

Notes

Cow Production History

Cow ID		Date of Sale or Removal	
Description (Breed/color)			

				Sale Weight	
Cow's Sire		Sire Breed			
Cow's Dam		Dam Breed		Sale Price/lb	
Cow's Birth Date		Weaning Weight			
Purchase Date		Purchase Price		Total Value	

Individual Cow Production Record

Calving

	Year	Bull ID & Breed	Cow Age	Calf ID	Calf Birth Date	Calf Sex	Birth Weight	Calving Ease	Calving Interval Days
1									
2									
3									
4									
5									
6									
7									
8									

Weaning

	Weaning Weight	205 Adj Wt.
1		
2		
3		
4		
5		
6		
7		
8		

Yearling

	Yearling Weight	365 Adj Wt.
1		
2		
3		
4		
5		
6		
7		
8		

Pregnant Test

	Pregnant (P) or (O) Open	BCS
1		
2		
3		
4		
5		
6		
7		
8		

Cow Production History

Cow ID	
Description (Breed/color)	
Cow's Sire	Sire Breed
Cow's Dam	Dam Breed
Cow's Birth Date	Weaning Weight
Purchase Date	Purchase Price

Date of Sale or Removal	
Sale Weight	
Sale Price/lb	
Total Value	

Individual Cow Production Record

Calving

	Year	Bull ID & Breed	Cow Age	Calf ID	Calf Birth Date	Calf Sex	Birth Weight	Calving Ease	Calving Interval Days
1									
2									
3									
4									
5									
6									
7									
8									

	Weaning		Yearling		Pregnant Test	
	Weaning Weight	205 Adj Wt.	Yearling Weight	365 Adj Wt.	Pregnant (P) or (O) Open	BCS
1						
2						
3						
4						
5						
6						
7						
8						

Notes

Notes

Cow Production History

Cow ID

Description (Breed/color)

Cow's Sire	Sire Breed	
Cow's Dam	Dam Breed	
Cow's Birth Date	Weaning Weight	
Purchase Date	Purchase Price	

Date of Sale or Removal	
Sale Weight	
Sale Price/lb	
Total Value	

Individual Cow Production Record

Calving

	Year	Bull ID & Breed	Cow Age	Calf ID	Calf Birth Date	Calf Sex	Birth Weight	Calving Ease	Calving Interval Days
1									
2									
3									
4									
5									
6									
7									
8									

Weaning

	Weaning Weight	205 Adj Wt.
1		
2		
3		
4		
5		
6		
7		
8		

Yearling

	Yearling Weight	365 Adj Wt.
1		
2		
3		
4		
5		
6		
7		
8		

Pregnant Test

	Pregnant (P) or (O) Open	BCS
1		
2		
3		
4		
5		
6		
7		
8		

Cow Production History

Cow ID		Date of Sale or Removal	
Description (Breed/color)			
Cow's Sire	Sire Breed	Sale Weight	
Cow's Dam	Dam Breed	Sale Price/lb	
Cow's Birth Date	Weaning Weight		
Purchase Date	Purchase Price	Total Value	

Individual Cow Production Record

Calving

	Year	Bull ID & Breed	Cow Age	Calf ID	Calf Birth Date	Calf Sex	Birth Weight	Calving Ease	Calving Interval Days
1									
2									
3									
4									
5									
6									
7									
8									

Weaning

	Weaning Weight	205 Adj Wt.
1		
2		
3		
4		
5		
6		
7		
8		

Yearling

	Yearling Weight	365 Adj Wt.
1		
2		
3		
4		
5		
6		
7		
8		

Pregnant Test

	Pregnant (P) or (O) Open	BCS
1		
2		
3		
4		
5		
6		
7		
8		

Notes

Notes

Cow Production History

Cow ID	
Description (Breed/color)	

Cow's Sire		Sire Breed	
Cow's Dam		Dam Breed	
Cow's Birth Date		Weaning Weight	
Purchase Date		Purchase Price	

Date of Sale or Removal	
Sale Weight	
Sale Price/lb	
Total Value	

Individual Cow Production Record

Calving

	Year	Bull ID & Breed	Cow Age	Calf ID	Calf Birth Date	Calf Sex	Birth Weight	Calving Ease	Calving Interval Days
1									
2									
3									
4									
5									
6									
7									
8									

Weaning

	Weaning Weight	205 Adj Wt.
1		
2		
3		
4		
5		
6		
7		
8		

Yearling

	Yearling Weight	365 Adj Wt.
1		
2		
3		
4		
5		
6		
7		
8		

Pregnant Test

	Pregnant (P) or (O) Open	BCS
1		
2		
3		
4		
5		
6		
7		
8		

Cow Production History

Cow ID			Date of Sale or Removal	
Description (Breed/color)				
Cow's Sire		Sire Breed	Sale Weight	
Cow's Dam		Dam Breed	Sale Price/lb	
Cow's Birth Date		Weaning Weight		
Purchase Date		Purchase Price	Total Value	

Individual Cow Production Record

Calving

	Year	Bull ID & Breed	Cow Age	Calf ID	Calf Birth Date	Calf Sex	Birth Weight	Calving Ease	Calving Interval Days
1									
2									
3									
4									
5									
6									
7									
8									

Weaning

	Weaning Weight	205 Adj Wt.
1		
2		
3		
4		
5		
6		
7		
8		

Yearling

	Yearling Weight	365 Adj Wt.
1		
2		
3		
4		
5		
6		
7		
8		

Pregnant Test

	Pregnant (P) or (O) Open	BCS
1		
2		
3		
4		
5		
6		
7		
8		

Notes

Notes

Cow Production History

Cow ID

Description (Breed/color)

Cow's Sire   Sire Breed

Cow's Dam   Dam Breed

Cow's Birth Date   Weaning Weight

Purchase Date   Purchase Price

Date of Sale or Removal	
Sale Weight	
Sale Price/lb	
Total Value	

Individual Cow Production Record

Calving

	Year	Bull ID & Breed	Cow Age	Calf ID	Calf Birth Date	Calf Sex	Birth Weight	Calving Ease	Calving Interval Days
1									
2									
3									
4									
5									
6									
7									
8									

Weaning

	Weaning Weight	205 Adj Wt.
1		
2		
3		
4		
5		
6		
7		
8		

Yearling

	Yearling Weight	365 Adj Wt.
1		
2		
3		
4		
5		
6		
7		
8		

Pregnant Test

	Pregnant (P) or (O) Open	BCS
1		
2		
3		
4		
5		
6		
7		
8		

Cow Production History

Cow ID		Date of Sale or Removal	

Description (Breed/color)			
Cow's Sire	Sire Breed	Sale Weight	
Cow's Dam	Dam Breed	Sale Price/lb	
Cow's Birth Date	Weaning Weight	Total Value	
Purchase Date	Purchase Price		

Individual Cow Production Record

Calving

	Year	Bull ID & Breed	Cow Age	Calf ID	Calf Birth Date	Calf Sex	Birth Weight	Calving Ease	Calving Interval Days
1									
2									
3									
4									
5									
6									
7									
8									

	Weaning		Yearling		Pregnant Test	
	Weaning Weight	205 Adj Wt.	Yearling Weight	365 Adj Wt.	Pregnant (P) or (O) Open	BCS
1						
2						
3						
4						
5						
6						
7						
8						

Notes

Notes

Cow Production History

Cow ID		Date of Sale or Removal	
Description (Breed/color)		Sale Weight	
Cow's Sire	Sire Breed	Sale Price/lb	
Cow's Dam	Dam Breed		
Cow's Birth Date	Weaning Weight	Total Value	
Purchase Date	Purchase Price		

Individual Cow Production Record

Calving

	Year	Bull ID & Breed	Cow Age	Calf ID	Calf Birth Date	Calf Sex	Birth Weight	Calving Ease	Calving Interval Days
1									
2									
3									
4									
5									
6									
7									
8									

Weaning

	Weaning Weight	205 Adj Wt.
1		
2		
3		
4		
5		
6		
7		
8		

Yearling

	Yearling Weight	365 Adj Wt.
1		
2		
3		
4		
5		
6		
7		
8		

Pregnant Test

	Pregnant (P) or (O) Open	BCS
1		
2		
3		
4		
5		
6		
7		
8		

Cow Production History

Cow ID | [   ]

Description (Breed/color) | [   ]

		Date of Sale or Removal	
Cow's Sire		Sire Breed	
Cow's Dam		Dam Breed	
Cow's Birth Date		Weaning Weight	
Purchase Date		Purchase Price	

Sale Weight	
Sale Price/lb	
Total Value	

Individual Cow Production Record

Calving

	Year	Bull ID & Breed	Cow Age	Calf ID	Calf Birth Date	Calf Sex	Birth Weight	Calving Ease	Calving Interval Days
1									
2									
3									
4									
5									
6									
7									
8									

Weaning

	Weaning Weight	205 Adj Wt.
1		
2		
3		
4		
5		
6		
7		
8		

Yearling

	Yearling Weight	365 Adj Wt.
1		
2		
3		
4		
5		
6		
7		
8		

Pregnant Test

	Pregnant (P) or (O) Open	BCS
1		
2		
3		
4		
5		
6		
7		
8		

Notes

Notes

Cow Production History

Cow ID [   ]

Description (Breed/color) [   ]

Cow's Sire [   ] Sire Breed [   ]

Cow's Dam [   ] Dam Breed [   ]

Cow's Birth Date [   ] Weaning Weight [   ]

Purchase Date [   ] Purchase Price [   ]

Date of Sale or Removal	
Sale Weight	
Sale Price/lb	
Total Value	

Individual Cow Production Record

Calving

	Year	Bull ID & Breed	Cow Age	Calf ID	Calf Birth Date	Calf Sex	Birth Weight	Calving Ease	Calving Interval Days
1									
2									
3									
4									
5									
6									
7									
8									

Weaning

	Weaning Weight	205 Adj Wt.
1		
2		
3		
4		
5		
6		
7		
8		

Yearling

	Yearling Weight	365 Adj Wt.
1		
2		
3		
4		
5		
6		
7		
8		

Pregnant Test

	Pregnant (P) or (O) Open	BCS
1		
2		
3		
4		
5		
6		
7		
8		

Cow Production History

Cow ID _____

Description (Breed/color) _____

Cow's Sire		Sire Breed	
Cow's Dam		Dam Breed	
Cow's Birth Date		Weaning Weight	
Purchase Date		Purchase Price	

Date of Sale or Removal	
Sale Weight	
Sale Price/lb	
Total Value	

Individual Cow Production Record

Calving

	Year	Bull ID & Breed	Cow Age	Calf ID	Calf Birth Date	Calf Sex	Birth Weight	Calving Ease	Calving Interval Days
1									
2									
3									
4									
5									
6									
7									
8									

Weaning

	Weaning Weight	205 Adj Wt.
1		
2		
3		
4		
5		
6		
7		
8		

Yearling

	Yearling Weight	365 Adj Wt.
1		
2		
3		
4		
5		
6		
7		
8		

Pregnant Test

	Pregnant (P) or (O) Open	BCS
1		
2		
3		
4		
5		
6		
7		
8		

Notes

Notes

Cow Production History

Cow ID [＿＿＿＿＿＿＿＿＿＿＿＿＿＿＿]

Description (Breed/color) [＿＿＿＿＿＿＿＿＿＿]

Cow's Sire [＿＿＿]	Sire Breed [＿＿＿]	
Cow's Dam [＿＿＿]	Dam Breed [＿＿＿]	
Cow's Birth Date [＿＿＿]	Weaning Weight [＿＿＿]	
Purchase Date [＿＿＿]	Purchase Price [＿＿＿]	

Date of Sale or Removal	
Sale Weight	
Sale Price/lb	
Total Value	

Individual Cow Production Record

Calving

	Year	Bull ID & Breed	Cow Age	Calf ID	Calf Birth Date	Calf Sex	Birth Weight	Calving Ease	Calving Interval Days
1									
2									
3									
4									
5									
6									
7									
8									

Weaning

	Weaning Weight	205 Adj Wt.
1		
2		
3		
4		
5		
6		
7		
8		

Yearling

	Yearling Weight	365 Adj Wt.
1		
2		
3		
4		
5		
6		
7		
8		

Pregnant Test

	Pregnant (P) or (O) Open	BCS
1		
2		
3		
4		
5		
6		
7		
8		

Cow Production History

Cow ID		Date of Sale or Removal	
Description (Breed/color)		Sale Weight	
Cow's Sire	Sire Breed	Sale Price/lb	
Cow's Dam	Dam Breed		
Cow's Birth Date	Weaning Weight	Total Value	
Purchase Date	Purchase Price		

Individual Cow Production Record

Calving

	Year	Bull ID & Breed	Cow Age	Calf ID	Calf Birth Date	Calf Sex	Birth Weight	Calving Ease	Calving Interval Days
1									
2									
3									
4									
5									
6									
7									
8									

Weaning / Yearling / Pregnant Test

	Weaning Weight	205 Adj Wt.	Yearling Weight	365 Adj Wt.	Pregnant (P) or (O) Open	BCS
1						
2						
3						
4						
5						
6						
7						
8						

Notes

Notes

Cow Production History

Cow ID		Date of Sale or Removal	
Description (Breed/color)		Sale Weight	
Cow's Sire	Sire Breed	Sale Price/lb	
Cow's Dam	Dam Breed		
Cow's Birth Date	Weaning Weight	Total Value	
Purchase Date	Purchase Price		

Individual Cow Production Record

Calving

	Year	Bull ID & Breed	Cow Age	Calf ID	Calf Birth Date	Calf Sex	Birth Weight	Calving Ease	Calving Interval Days
1									
2									
3									
4									
5									
6									
7									
8									

Weaning

	Weaning Weight	205 Adj Wt.
1		
2		
3		
4		
5		
6		
7		
8		

Yearling

	Yearling Weight	365 Adj Wt.
1		
2		
3		
4		
5		
6		
7		
8		

Pregnant Test

	Pregnant (P) or (O) Open	BCS
1		
2		
3		
4		
5		
6		
7		
8		

Cow Production History

Cow ID		Date of Sale or Removal	
Description (Breed/color)		Sale Weight	
Cow's Sire	Sire Breed		
Cow's Dam	Dam Breed	Sale Price/lb	
Cow's Birth Date	Weaning Weight		
Purchase Date	Purchase Price	Total Value	

Individual Cow Production Record

Calving

	Year	Bull ID & Breed	Cow Age	Calf ID	Calf Birth Date	Calf Sex	Birth Weight	Calving Ease	Calving Interval Days
1									
2									
3									
4									
5									
6									
7									
8									

Weaning

	Weaning Weight	205 Adj Wt.
1		
2		
3		
4		
5		
6		
7		
8		

Yearling

	Yearling Weight	365 Adj Wt.
1		
2		
3		
4		
5		
6		
7		
8		

Pregnant Test

	Pregnant (P) or (O) Open	BCS
1		
2		
3		
4		
5		
6		
7		
8		

Notes

Notes

Cow Production History

Cow ID	
Description (Breed/color)	
Cow's Sire	Sire Breed
Cow's Dam	Dam Breed
Cow's Birth Date	Weaning Weight
Purchase Date	Purchase Price

Date of Sale or Removal	
Sale Weight	
Sale Price/lb	
Total Value	

Individual Cow Production Record

Calving

	Year	Bull ID & Breed	Cow Age	Calf ID	Calf Birth Date	Calf Sex	Birth Weight	Calving Ease	Calving Interval Days
1									
2									
3									
4									
5									
6									
7									
8									

Weaning

	Weaning Weight	205 Adj Wt.
1		
2		
3		
4		
5		
6		
7		
8		

Yearling

	Yearling Weight	365 Adj Wt.
1		
2		
3		
4		
5		
6		
7		
8		

Pregnant Test

	Pregnant (P) or (O) Open	BCS
1		
2		
3		
4		
5		
6		
7		
8		

Cow Production History

Cow ID	
Description (Breed/color)	
Cow's Sire	Sire Breed
Cow's Dam	Dam Breed
Cow's Birth Date	Weaning Weight
Purchase Date	Purchase Price

Date of Sale or Removal	
Sale Weight	
Sale Price/lb	
Total Value	

Individual Cow Production Record

Calving

	Year	Bull ID & Breed	Cow Age	Calf ID	Calf Birth Date	Calf Sex	Birth Weight	Calving Ease	Calving Interval Days
1									
2									
3									
4									
5									
6									
7									
8									

Weaning

	Weaning Weight	205 Adj Wt.
1		
2		
3		
4		
5		
6		
7		
8		

Yearling

	Yearling Weight	365 Adj Wt.
1		
2		
3		
4		
5		
6		
7		
8		

Pregnant Test

	Pregnant (P) or (O) Open	BCS
1		
2		
3		
4		
5		
6		
7		
8		

Notes

Notes

LIVESTOCK EXPENSE
Record

Livestock Expense Record

Expense Item						Amount
Date	Description	Feed	Supplies	Medical	Other	
Total project(s) Expenses						=
Net Profit or Loss						
"Total Income Minus Total Expenses."						=

Livestock Expense Record

Expense Item						Amount
Date	Description	Feed	Supplies	Medical	Other	
Total project(s) Expenses						=
Net Profit or Loss						
"Total Income Minus Total Expenses."						=

Livestock Expense Record

Expense Item						Amount
Date	Description	Feed	Supplies	Medical	Other	
Total project(s) Expenses						=
Net Profit or Loss						
"Total Income Minus Total Expenses."						=

Livestock Expense Record

Expense Item						Amount
Date	Description	Feed	Supplies	Medical	Other	
Total project(s) Expenses						=
Net Profit or Loss						
"Total Income Minus Total Expenses."						=

Livestock Expense Record

Expense Item						Amount
Date	Description	Feed	Supplies	Medical	Other	
Total project(s) Expenses						**=**
Net Profit or Loss						
"Total Income Minus Total Expenses."						**=**

Livestock Expense Record

Expense Item						Amount
Date	Description	Feed	Supplies	Medical	Other	
Total project(s) Expenses						**=**
Net Profit or Loss						
"Total Income Minus Total Expenses."						**=**

Livestock Expense Record

Expense Item						Amount
Date	Description	Feed	Supplies	Medical	Other	
Total project(s) Expenses						=
Net Profit or Loss						
"Total Income Minus Total Expenses."						=

Livestock Expense Record

Expense Item						Amount
Date	Description	Feed	Supplies	Medical	Other	
Total project(s) Expenses						=
Net Profit or Loss						
"Total Income Minus Total Expenses."						=

Livestock Expense Record

Expense Item						Amount
Date	Description	Feed	Supplies	Medical	Other	
Total project(s) Expenses						=
Net Profit or Loss						
"Total Income Minus Total Expenses."						=

Livestock Expense Record

Expense Item						Amount
Date	Description	Feed	Supplies	Medical	Other	
Total project(s) Expenses						=
Net Profit or Loss						
"Total Income Minus Total Expenses."						=

Livestock Expense Record

Expense Item						Amount
Date	Description	Feed	Supplies	Medical	Other	
Total project(s) Expenses						**=**
Net Profit or Loss						
"Total Income Minus Total Expenses."						**=**

Livestock Expense Record

Expense Item						Amount
Date	Description	Feed	Supplies	Medical	Other	
Total project(s) Expenses						**=**
Net Profit or Loss						
"Total Income Minus Total Expenses."						**=**

Livestock Expense Record

Expense Item						Amount
Date	Description	Feed	Supplies	Medical	Other	
Total project(s) Expenses						**=**
Net Profit or Loss						
"Total Income Minus Total Expenses."						**=**

Livestock Expense Record

Expense Item						Amount
Date	Description	Feed	Supplies	Medical	Other	
Total project(s) Expenses						**=**
Net Profit or Loss						
"Total Income Minus Total Expenses."						**=**

Livestock Expense Record

		Expense Item				Amount
Date	Description	Feed	Supplies	Medical	Other	
Total project(s) Expenses						=
Net Profit or Loss						
"Total Income Minus Total Expenses."						=

Livestock Expense Record

Expense Item						Amount
Date	Description	Feed	Supplies	Medical	Other	
Total project(s) Expenses						**=**
Net Profit or Loss						
"Total Income Minus Total Expenses."						**=**

Livestock Expense Record

Expense Item						Amount
Date	Description	Feed	Supplies	Medical	Other	
Total project(s) Expenses						**=**
Net Profit or Loss						
"Total Income Minus Total Expenses."						**=**

Livestock Expense Record

Expense Item						Amount
Date	Description	Feed	Supplies	Medical	Other	
Total project(s) Expenses						**=**
Net Profit or Loss						
"Total Income Minus Total Expenses."						**=**

Livestock Expense Record

Expense Item						Amount
Date	Description	Feed	Supplies	Medical	Other	
Total project(s) Expenses						=
Net Profit or Loss						
"Total Income Minus Total Expenses."						=

Livestock Expense Record

Expense Item						Amount
Date	Description	Feed	Supplies	Medical	Other	
Total project(s) Expenses						**=**
Net Profit or Loss						
"Total Income Minus Total Expenses."						**=**

Hi Dear

We are so thrilled you've chosen to purchase COW CALF RECORD BOOK from us,
We hope you love it! If you do, would you consider posting an online review
on AMAZON! This helps us to continue providing great products
and helps potential buyers to make confident decisions,

Thank you in advance for your review and for being a preferred customer!

Mo Elka